A Special
Christmas
Blessing

...Just for You

A Special Christmas Blessing

...Just for You

Douglas Pagels

Blue Mountain Press ™
Boulder, Colorado

Library of Congress Control Number: 2013937574
ISBN: 978-1-59842-757-8 (Blue Mountain Arts edition)
ISBN: 978-1-59842-753-0 (Barnes & Noble edition)

◾ and Blue Mountain Press are registered in U.S. Patent and Trademark Office. Certain trademarks are used under license.

Printed in China.
First Printing: 2013

Blue Mountain Arts, Inc.
P.O. Box 4549, Boulder, Colorado 80306

I want to wish you
everything that
could ever bring
a smile to your life.

May Your Days Be Filled with Blessings!

I want your life to be such a
  wonderful one.
I wish you peace, deep within your soul;
joyfulness in the promise of each new day;
stars to reach for, dreams to come true,
and memories more beautiful than
  words can say...

I wish you friends close at heart,
even over the miles;
loved ones ~ the best treasures
we're blessed with;
present moments to live in,
one day at a time.

I wish you serenity, with its wisdom;
courage, with its strength;
and new beginnings, to give life a
chance to really shine.

I wish you understanding ~
    of how special you really are;
a journey, safe from the storms and
    warmed by the sun;
a path to wonderful things;
an invitation to the abundance
    life brings;
and an angel watching over,
    for all the days to come.

Everyone should have a Christmas wish list for the special people in their lives. Here are some of the things I'll be wishing for you...

I want the kind of joy that you always give to others... to come back and bless you all throughout the year.

And I want you to be reminded from time to time that you are a wonderful gift and one of the nicest things in this entire world... is your presence in it.

Have a Merry Christmas and a Very Happy Year to Come

I want to wish you a Christmas that is the most wonderful one you've ever had!

As the beauty of this magical season begins to shine all around you, I'd love it if you would keep on remembering this...

I think you are one of the truly special people in this world. You're one of the finest people I'll ever know, and the wishes I have for you are ones that will be wished for you far beyond today.

I hope your life is filled with
the precious kind of joy you
give to others and with the
priceless kind of gifts everyone
wishes that they could give to you.

Gifts like... the thanks of friends
and loved ones who are so glad
that you are here.

And presents like... hope and
happiness in every day of
the year ahead.

May You Always Have
an Angel
by Your Side

May you always have an angel
by your side ◞ Watching out for
you in all the things you do ◞
Reminding you to keep believing
in brighter days ◞ Finding ways
for your wishes and dreams to take
you to beautiful places ◞ Giving
you hope that is as certain as the
sun ◞ Giving you the strength of
serenity as your guide...

May you always have love and comfort
and courage  And may you always have
an angel by your side  Someone there to
catch you if you fall  Encouraging your
dreams  Inspiring your happiness  Holding
your hand and helping you through it all

In all of our days, our lives are always
changing  Tears come along as well as smiles

Along the roads you travel, may the miles
be a thousand times more lovely than lonely ⚜
May they give you gifts that never, ever end:
someone wonderful to love and a dear friend
in whom you can confide ⚜ May you have
rainbows after every storm ⚜ May you have
hopes to keep you warm ⚜

And may you always have
an angel by your side ⚜

I Want You to Remember That All These Things Are True About You

You are something ~ and someone ~ very special. You really are. No one else in this entire world is exactly like you, and there are so many remarkable things about you...

You're a one-of-a-kind treasure, uniquely here in this space and time. You are here to shine in your own wonderful way, sharing your smile in the best way you can, and remembering all the while that a little light somewhere makes a brighter light everywhere. You can ~ and you do ~ make a wonderful contribution to this world.

You have qualities within you that many people would love to have, and those who really and truly know you... are so glad that they do. You have a big heart and a good and sensitive soul.

You are gifted with thoughts and ways of seeing things that only special people know. You know that life doesn't always play by the rules, but that in the long run, everything will work out.

You understand that you and your actions are capable of turning anything around ~ and that joys once lost can always be found. There is a resolve and an inner reserve of strength in you that few ever get to see. You have so many treasures within ~ those you're only beginning to discover, and all the ones you're already aware of.

Never forget what a treasure you are.
That special person in the mirror may not
always get to hear all the compliments you
so sweetly deserve, but you are so worthy
of such an abundance
...of friendship, joy, and love.

Presents That Don't Fit Under the Tree

I wish you... an abundance of happiness. Feelings that warm your world and make you smile. Friends and loved ones by your side... people who are going to treasure every memory they get to make with you.

Wonderful surprises in your life. Beautiful sunrises in your days. Opportunities that come along. Chances you've hoped for. Goals you've been striving to reach. Changes you've wanted to make.

A song in your heart. A wish that comes true. And reminders of how much nicer this world is... because of you.

Always Be Hope~Full

To have hope in your life is exactly what it's like for a December night to have stars in the sky.

It's a brilliant way to be.

A Holiday Message to You... from Me

There are a few absolute gems in this world. They are the people who make a tremendous difference in other people's lives... with the smiles they give, the blessings they share, and the way they warm the hearts of everyone around them.

These rare and remarkable people are so deserving of every hope and happiness. They are the people who are incredibly unique, enormously thanked, and endlessly appreciated for everything they do.

And one of those wonderful, deserving, and one-of-a-kind people is most definitely... you.

I wish you guiding lights and
joy and faith and wishes on a star.

And I hope you'll never forget...
   for even a day...
      how very special you are.

I Want to Wish You
Moments like This

Life is not measured by the number
of breaths we take, but by the moments
that take our breath away.

~ Anonymous

You are so deserving of every good thing that can come your way. And I want you to know, if I could have a Christmas wish come true, I'd wish for every day of your life to be blessed with some special gift that warms your heart, some wonderful smile that touches your soul, and so many things that simply take your breath away.

Every day is a present we are given. Every sunrise comes along to shine in our lives, bring us new opportunities, and help us have a better understanding of who we can be and what we can achieve.

The best thing to do with the present... is untie the ribbons, discover the blessings, and make the most of everything the new day brings.

May a gently falling snow nestle against the windows of your dreams on Christmas Eve, and may your silent night be warmed by the thought that the gifts of peace and goodwill may someday come to us all.

May you imagine a time when anyone having difficult days will be able to see their way through, and may the whole world wake up on Christmas morning to discover... that some dreams really do come true.

May the days ahead inspire so many smiles in your life!

May this season fill your world with joy and encouragement. May you remember my prayer for you... a precious thought that everywhere you go, people will lovingly know how much there is to appreciate about you.

Special Christmas Gifts
I Wish for You

Happiness. Deep down within.
Serenity. With each sunrise.
Success. In each facet of your life.
Close and caring friends.
Love. That never ends.

Special memories. Of all the yesterdays.

A bright today. With much to be
thankful for.

A path. That leads to beautiful tomorrows.

Dreams. That do their best to come true.

And appreciation. Of all the wonderful
things about you.

I Just Want to Make Sure You Know This

Your kindness, your caring, the way you brighten the lives of everyone around you... those things are the things that help to make the world so much nicer.

I feel very blessed to have you in my life, and I'd love it if you would remember

    what a special place

        you'll always have

           ...in my heart.

A Special Blessing to Remember in the Serenity of the Season

It's not a monumental, once-in-a-lifetime moment that comes along and brings us happiness.

What fills our hearts with quiet joy and puts smiles on our faces are all the little things we do on a daily basis. The little things in life are really the big things. And the simplest things are very often the sweetest things.

Our present moments are some of our most priceless gifts. We are blessed with so much in our daily lives, and all the small, special things that lift us up a little higher can never be taken for granted.

It truly is in the simple, little things where the possibilities arise, where the light shines brightest, and where the sweetest serenity is found.

Thoughts About New Years and New Beginnings

I know you might be wondering what will happen in the next chapter of your life.

If there are any changes to deal with in the year ahead, there's no better advice than this: just do your best. Make sure you stay strong enough to move ahead because there are some wonderful rewards waiting for you...

It won't all make sense right away, but I promise you: over the course of time, answers will come, decisions will prove to be the right ones, and the path will be easier to see. Here are some things you can do that will help to see you through...

You can have hope. Because it works wonders for those who have it. You can be optimistic. Because people who expect things to turn out for the best often set the stage to receive a beautiful result.

You can put things in perspective. Because some things are important, and others are definitely not.

You can remember that beyond the clouds the sun is still shining. You can meet each challenge and give it all you've got.

You can count your blessings. You can be inspired to climb your ladders and have some nice, long talks with your wishing stars. You can be strong and patient. You can be gentle and wise.

And you can believe in happy endings. Because you are the author of the story of your life.

May you have feelings that are
shared from heart to heart,
simple pleasures amidst this
complex world, and goals that
are within your grasp.

I want you to keep planting the
seeds of your dreams... because if
you keep believing in them,
they'll keep trying their best
to blossom for you.

Don't Ever Stop Dreaming Your Dreams

Don't ever try to understand everything ~
   some things will just never make sense.
Don't ever be reluctant
      to show your feelings ~
      when you're happy, give in to it!
   When you're not, live with it.
Don't ever be afraid to try to
      make things better ~
      you might be surprised at the results.
Don't ever take the weight of the world
   on your shoulders.

Don't ever feel threatened by the future ~
    take life one day at a time.
Don't ever feel guilty about the past ~
    what's done is done. Learn from any
    mistakes you might have made.
Don't ever feel that you are alone ~
    there is always somebody there for you
    to reach out to.
Don't ever forget that you can achieve
    so many of the things you can imagine ~
    imagine that! It's not as hard as it seems.
Don't ever stop loving,
    don't ever stop believing,
        don't ever stop dreaming your dreams.

I Hope This Will Bring the Blessing of Encouragement to You...

May you remember that
though the roads we take can
sometimes be difficult,
those are often the ones that
lead to the most beautiful views.

I Wish You...

A thankful heart. Filled with friendship
and love.

Memories. You'll treasure forever.

Faith and courage. To rise above.

And reminders. Of how special you are.

Joy. To give you twinkles in your eyes.
Blessings. From angels in disguise.
Health and hope. On this journey
through life.
And the very best. Of everything!

I want the things you do to
turn into the nicest memories
any person could ever ask for.

May you go beyond the ordinary
steps and discover extraordinary
results. May you keep on trying to
reach for your stars, and may you
never forget how amazing you are.

May the days be good to you: comforting more often than crazy... and giving more often than taking.

May the passing seasons make sure that any heartaches are replaced with a thousand smiles and that any hard journeys eventually turn into nice, easy miles that take you everywhere you want to go.

Always stay strong, fight on, and be brave.
When things get a little too overwhelming,
remember that there is a better day on the
way, and it's just a matter of time... before
it brightens up your life and makes everything
right again.

I want you to be truly happy.
To discover some more sweetness
within the days. To be given some
more serenity. To search out more
rainbows. To find some more time
that is yours to spend as wisely and
as wonderfully as you can.

I Wish You Lasting Happiness

One of the secrets of happiness is to take time to accomplish what you have to do, then to make time to achieve what you want to do.

Remember that life is short. Its golden moments need hopes and memories and dreams. When it seems like those things are lost in the shuffle, you owe it to yourself to find them again. The days are too precious to let them slip away.

Find time, make time, take time... to do something rewarding and deeply personal and completely worthwhile. Time is your fortune, and you can spend it to bring more joy to yourself and to others your whole life through.

After the Holidays, Be Sure to Remember...

Sometimes it's important to work for that pot of gold.

But other times it's essential to take time off and to make sure that your most important decision in the day simply consists of choosing which color to slide down on the rainbow.

May Your Winter Hopes and Dreams Bring Joy to Everything

May you never lose your
sense of wonder, and may
you hold on to the sense
of humor you use to brighten
the lives of everyone
who knows you.

May you always be patient
with the problems of life and
know that any clouds will
eventually give way to the
sunlight of your most
hoped-for days. May you be
rewarded with the type of
friendships that get better and
better ~ and the kind of love
that blesses your life forever.

If I Could Have
a Wish Come True...

I would wish for nothing but
wonderful things to come to you.

In your life, which is so precious to me,
may troubles, worries, and problems
never linger; may they only make you
that much stronger and able and wise.

And may you rise each day with sunlight
in your heart, success in your path,
answers to your prayers,
    and that smile
        ~ that I love to see ~
           always there... in your eyes.

The Gift-Wrapped Present

Just like a wonderful Christmas present,
every morning comes to us gift-wrapped...
and fresh out of the box are moments we've
never experienced before, opportunities
we've never known, and new paths we've
never taken.

What a truly magnificent gift! Some people
have a hard time seeing the possibilities...
and they just let the chances slip away.
But those who understand the value of
the gift?

They have the chance to turn the present...
into a truly extraordinary day.

I Wish You the Best of Everything

These special words will always be here for you to turn to... for happiness, hope, and comfort. Here are some of the most important things you can do... to see your way through anything that comes along...

When you're counting your blessings, be
sure to include the privilege of having a new
sunrise every morning and a brand-new
beginning every day.

Don't ever give up on your hopes and
dreams. Your happiness is depending on
you to stay strong.

Know that you can reach deep inside and find everything you need to get through each moment that lies ahead.

So unwind a little and smile a lot and try not to worry too much. Know that you're loved and cared for... and that, whenever you need them, your guardian angels are great about working overtime.

May you always remember
that there are so many admirable,
one-of-a-kind things about you.
And may you never forget
that if you can search within and
find a smile... that smile will
always be a reflection of the way
people, like me, feel about you.

A Christmas Thanks
to You for Being
So Wonderful!

Has anyone ever told you what a
wonderful person you are?

I hope so! I hope you've been
   told dozens of times...
      because you are amazing,

And just in case you haven't heard
those words in a while,
I want you to hear them now.

You deserve to know that...

It takes someone special to do
what you do. It takes someone
rare and remarkable to make the
lives of everyone around them
nicer, brighter, and more beautiful.
It takes someone who has a big
heart and a caring soul. It takes
someone who's living proof of how
precious a person can be.

It takes someone... just like you.

A Blessing to Bring You a Smile Every Day

Nothing ever has and no one ever will compare with you. You deserve to be happy, to love yourself, and to be able to live your very best life... every day.

Don't ever believe anyone who tells you otherwise. You matter immensely. Your wishes are so important...

Your hopes and dreams are valid and valuable. And your inner strength is more powerful than you can imagine.

Never give up on the things you want to come true. Take what you want to do and need to do... and reach for it.

Life has so much to give when you hope and love and live each day in the very best way you can. There are no limits to the good you can do and the smiles you can bring to your heart.

You deserve to have so many great things come your way. You are amazing and capable and just so exquisite.

And when it comes to a wonderful life, one that brings all the best things to you, I want you to know how much you deserve it.

Remember that some of the secret joys of living are not found by rushing from point A to point B, but by slowing down and inventing some imaginary letters along the way.

Gifts I Wish I Could Give You

The gift of knowing that it's people like you who make life so sweet... for people like me.

All your friends and loved ones, from close by and miles away, gathered together to celebrate the holidays.

Happiness that simply overflows... from memories made, peacefulness within, and the anticipation of so many good things to come.

Days that shine so bright and stars that come out at night and listen to everything your heart is hoping for.

And paths ahead that take you all the places you want to be and that bring you closer to all the wonderful things on your wish list.

I wish I could find a way
to let you know how much
nicer life is... with you here.

I want you to pat yourself
on the back and be glad
that you leave so many
smiles on people's faces.

May You Really Hear Sleigh Bells in the Snow

May you count your blessings, one by one, and come up with a list that just makes you grin.

I want you to listen to your heart. To hear what any frustrations have to say and to find a better way. To know what brings you smiles ~ the very best kind ~ the "this is what it's all about" kind.

I want you to reach out to the people you are close to and to find yourself in the places that mean the most to you.

May you have a strong belief in
yourself ~ one that will always make
a difference in your days.

May you never feel threatened by the
future or bothered by the past.

May you feel that each new day is a
gift you have been given. May you
open that gift with childlike anticipation
and close the door at the end of each day
with a prayerful appreciation.

May you create lasting
changes in your life and in the
way you want tomorrow to be.

I wish you sweet dreams. I want
you to have times when you feel
like singing and dancing and
laughing out loud.

In Celebration of Everything About You

I hope you feel enormously appreciated today... because you are!

To describe you as being "absolutely wonderful" and "incredibly special" doesn't even begin to convey all the admiration and appreciation I have for you.

The world is a nicer place with you in it,
and it is such a blessing to have you here...
in my life and in the lives of so many
others... brightening up so many days!

You're just the best, and this special time is
a great chance to tell you so. I know the
year ahead will be a good one for you, and
I hope the joys and dreams and things you
wish for... all come true.

I want you to have as much
happiness as tomorrow can
promise to anyone.

I want everything
to work out for you
just the way you want it to.

Stars...
Above and Below

I think it's true that people are a little bit like stars. There are millions of them to see, but there are always a few that shine brighter and more beautifully than all the others.

The people who warm your heart and bring you a smile... those are the kind you want your life to be blessed with. Those are the ones you just adore.

Of all the stars in the sky, you are one of the brightest. You are a very special light in lots of people's lives, and you are thanked for all the warmth and happiness you bring!

May the year you are about to
enter grant you the promise of
success that knows no bounds:
friendship and love, blessings
from above, and dreams you
never imagined would come true.

Things to Reflect On

Success is so much more than most people imagine it to be.

Success is the reward you receive for all the good things you do. It's looking forward to the day. It's having plans and wishes and goals to pursue. It's letting your heart say yes.

Success is having fun and being healthy and finding ways to stay sane in this crazy world of ours.

It's keeping the faith that you'll get where you want to go. It's knowing, even as you work away all those hours of the day, you're setting the stage for something wonderful around the corner.

Success isn't just at the end of the rainbow. It's also found in the little things you do every day. So keep chasing your dreams and don't stop until you catch them.

And be sure to enjoy each blessing along the way!

Remember the Blessing of Looking on the Bright Side

You are personally responsible for so much of the sunshine that brightens up your life. Optimists and gentle souls continually benefit from their very own versions of daylight saving time. They get extra hours of happiness and sunshine every day.

May You Be Given the Gift of Love in All Its Forms

Love is... what holds everything together. It's the ribbon around the gift of life.

Love of family and love of friends... is where everything beautiful begins.

Ask me how important my family is to me and how essential my friends are, and I'll tell you this simple truth... nothing else even comes close.

The incredibly special connections we have with others are the things that matter most of all.

Whether they're close by or miles away, distance can never diminish what kindred souls feel in their hearts.

And whether the time spent in each other's company is a little or a lot, every single moment is a present we're blessed with.

There is nothing more wonderful than telling the ones you cherish... how much they're loved and appreciated... every chance you get. There is no greater or more precious advice.

Love is what holds everything together.
It's the ribbon around the gift of life.

A life well lived is simply a compilation of days well spent.

Let your days bring abundance into your heart and soul. Let them sing in you and show you how to aim for the stars. Let them help you reach out to be...
all that you are.

Sweet, Simple Gratitude

In a season when you should be showered
with the best presents imaginable, I want
to thank you for everything you do.

The gifts you give everyone all through
the year ~ the ones that come from
your kind and caring heart ~ are priceless.

Thank you for so many big things ~ and a million little things ~ that help bring happiness into other people's lives.

You are such a joy to everyone who is fortunate enough to know you!

And I am so glad that I've had the privilege of being one of those lucky people.

May You Be Blessed with a Wonderful Year Ahead!

What amazing gifts the new year brings! An entire year's worth of wonderful opportunities, given to us one sunrise at a time.

Many of the moments ahead will be marvelously disguised as ordinary days, but each one of us has the chance to make something extraordinary out of them.

Each new day is a blank page in the diary of your life. Every day you're given a chance to determine what the words will say and how the story will unfold.

If you work it right, the story of your life will be a wonderful one. The more rewarding you can make each page, the more exquisite the entire book will be. And I would love for you to write a masterpiece.

I want you to have pages on understanding and tales of overcoming hardship. I want you to fill your story with romance, adventure, success, and laughter.

I want each chapter to reflect the gift that you are. As you go about your day, I want you to remember: goodness will be rewarded. Smiles will pay you back. Have fun. Find strength. Be truthful. Have faith. Don't focus on anything you lack.

Remember that people are the treasures in life and happiness is the real wealth. Have a diary that describes how you are doing your best, and...

The rest will take care of itself.

I wish you wondrous things that can't be tied up in ribbons and bows. I wish you thoughts that take you to magnificent places. I wish you togetherness and abundant happiness. I wish you soaring hopes for the days ahead and profound joys for the year that has been.

And I wish you quiet times all to yourself, when the grace of all that is good in your life is sweetly celebrated within.

And Now, as This Book Comes to a Close...

I want to thank you for giving everyone around you the gift of a nicer world to live in.

I hope you'll never forget how much I treasure just being in this world with you. And I love knowing that everyone else feels the same way I do.

To your friends, you are everything
a friend should be. And to your
family, I know you are dearly
loved and truly the best.

I hope the year ahead will take you
everywhere your wishes have always
wanted to go.

And I really hope that all your days
are as beautiful and as bright... as the
ones you inspire in other people's lives.

May You Be Blessed with All These Things...

A little more joy,
a little less stress,
a lot more recognition of
your wonderfulness.

Abundance in your life,
blessings in your days,
dreams that come true,
and hopes that stay.

A rainbow on the horizon,
an angel by your side...
and everything
that could ever bring
a smile to your life.

About the Author

Best-selling author and editor
Douglas Pagels has inspired
millions of readers with his
insights and his anthologies.
His books have sold over 3
million copies, and he is one of
the most quoted contemporary
writers on the Internet today.
Reflecting a philosophy that is
perfect for our times, Doug has
a wonderful knack for sharing
his thoughts and sentiments in
a voice that is so positive and
understanding we can't help
but take the message to heart.

His writings have been translated into over a dozen languages
due to their global appeal and inspiring outlook on life,
and his work has been quoted by many worthy causes and
charitable organizations.

He and his wife live in Colorado, and they are the parents of
children in college and beyond. Over the years, Doug has spent
much of his time as a classroom volunteer, a youth basketball
coach, an advocate for local environmental issues, a frequent
traveler, and a craftsman, building a cabin in the Rocky Mountains.